Hippopotamuses

by Rachel Grack

BLASTOFF!
READERS
2

BELLWETHER MEDIA • MINNEAPOLIS, MN

Note to Librarians, Teachers, and Parents:

Blastoff! Readers are carefully developed by literacy experts and combine standards-based content with developmentally appropriate text.

Level 1 provides the most support through repetition of high-frequency words, light text, predictable sentence patterns, and strong visual support.

Level 2 offers early readers a bit more challenge through varied simple sentences, increased text load, and less repetition of high-frequency words.

Level 3 advances early-fluent readers toward fluency through increased text and concept load, less reliance on visuals, longer sentences, and more literary language.

Level 4 builds reading stamina by providing more text per page, increased use of punctuation, greater variation in sentence patterns, and increasingly challenging vocabulary.

Level 5 encourages children to move from "learning to read" to "reading to learn" by providing even more text, varied writing styles, and less familiar topics.

Whichever book is right for your reader, Blastoff! Readers are the perfect books to build confidence and encourage a love of reading that will last a lifetime!

This edition first published in 2020 by Bellwether Media, Inc.

No part of this publication may be reproduced in whole or in part without written permission of the publisher. For information regarding permission, write to Bellwether Media, Inc., Attention: Permissions Department, 6012 Blue Circle Drive, Minnetonka, MN 55343.

Library of Congress Cataloging-in-Publication Data

Names: Koestler-Grack, Rachel A., 1973- author.
Title: Hippopotamuses / by Rachel Grack.
Description: Minneapolis, MN : Bellwether Media, Inc., 2020. | Series:
   Blastoff! Readers. Animals of the Wetlands | Audience: Age 5-8. |
   Audience: K to Grade 3. | Includes bibliographical references and index.
Identifiers: LCCN 2018051144 (print) | LCCN 2018051556 (ebook) | ISBN
   9781618915290 (ebook) | ISBN 9781626179899 (hardcover : alk. paper)
Subjects: LCSH: Hippopotamidae--Juvenile literature. | Wetland
   animals--Juvenile literature.
Classification: LCC QL737.U57 (ebook) | LCC QL737.U57 K64 2020 (print) | DDC
   599.63/5--dc23
LC record available at https://lccn.loc.gov/2018051144

Editor: Betsy Rathburn   Designer: Josh Brink

Printed in the United States of America, North Mankato, MN.

Table of Contents

Life in the Wetlands

Hippopotamuses are huge **mammals** that live in Africa. They **wallow** in lakes and slow-moving rivers.

4

Hippos have **adapted** well to the wetlands **biome**!

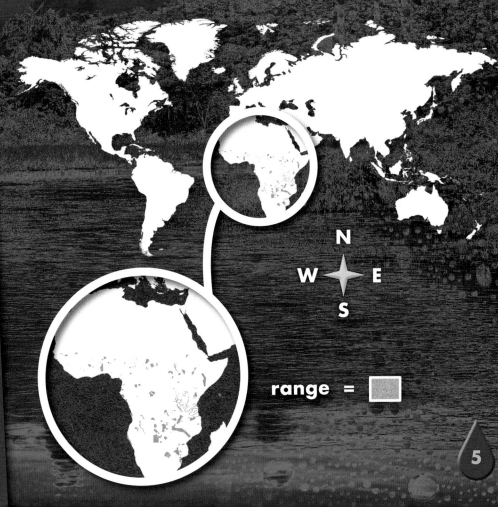

Hippopotamus Range

N
W E
S

range = ☐

African wetlands get hot!
Hippos stay cool underwater.

6

Their eyes, ears, and **nostrils** are on top of their heads. This means hippos can stay **submerged**.

nostrils

Clear inner eyelids help hippos see underwater. Their ears and noses close up to keep water out.

Hippos even sleep in the water!

Special Adaptations

red mucus

eyes, ears, and nostrils on top of head

clear inner eyelids

Hippo skin dries out quickly on land. It easily sunburns.

Hippos sometimes produce a red **mucus** called blood sweat. This keeps hippos safe in the sun!

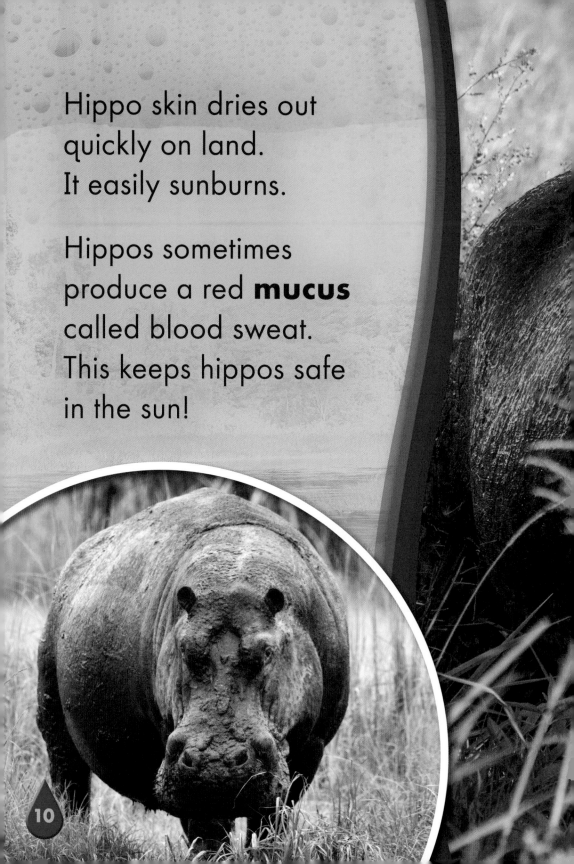

mucus

Sticking Together

bloat

Hippos live together in groups called **bloats**. Their most dangerous threats are other hippos!

Males **gape** their powerful jaws to scare away other males.

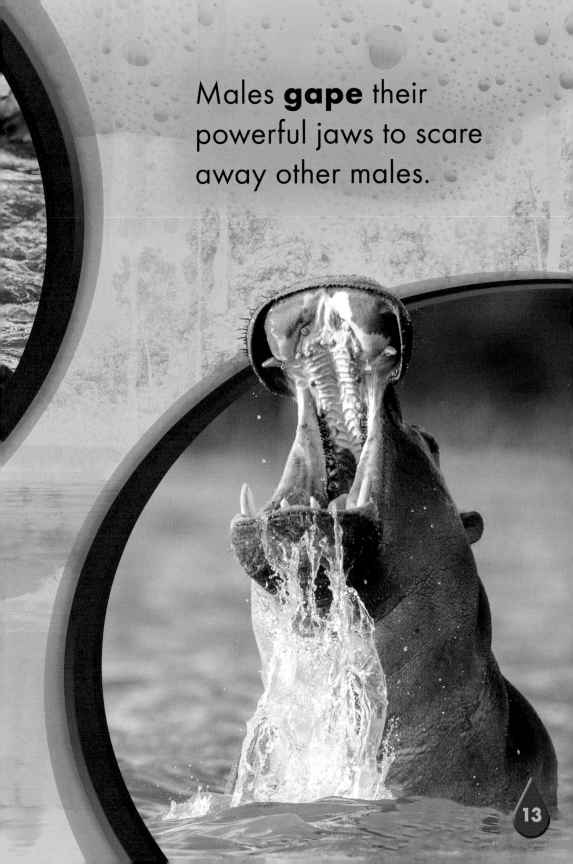

Female hippos nurse newborn **calves** in the water. This helps keep young safe from danger.

Calves learn to fight by playing with each other!

calves

Hippopotamus Stats

Least Concern	Near Threatened	Vulnerable	Endangered	Critically Endangered	Extinct in the Wild	Extinct

conservation status: vulnerable

life span: up to 50 years

Hippos **communicate** with grunts and wheezes. Loud calls warn others of danger.

16

Their **bellows** can be heard in the air and underwater!

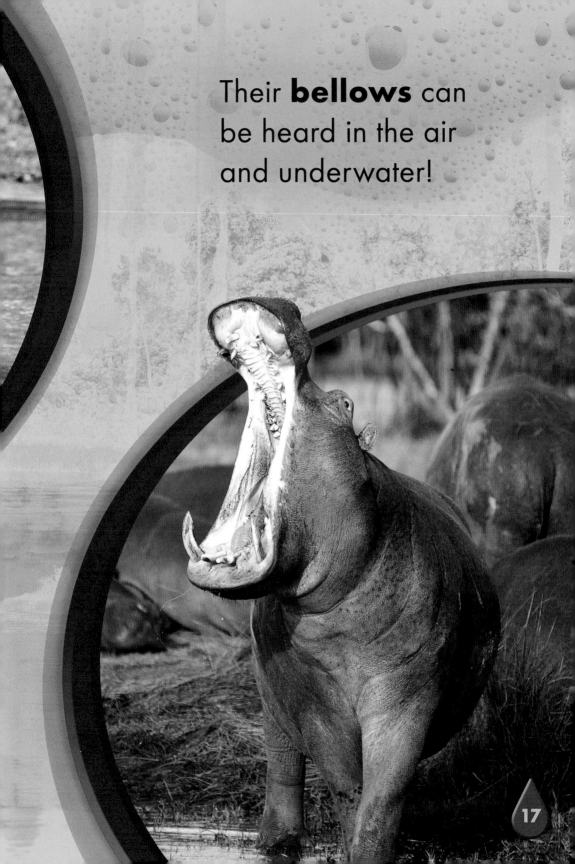

Hungry, Hungry Hippos

Hippos usually **graze** at night. Their strong lips grip and tear short grasses.

These **nocturnal** feeders can sniff out fallen fruit!

Hippopotamus Diet

scutch grass

green foxtail

papyrus sedge

tusks

Hippos have long, sharp
tusks. They sometimes
use them to fight.

Mighty hippos hardly ever share their **habitat**!

Glossary

adapted—changed over a long period of time

bellows—loud calls

biome—a large area with certain plants, animals, and weather

bloats—groups of hippos that live together

calves—baby hippos

communicate—to share information and feelings

gape—to open widely

graze—to feed on a field of grass

habitat—the place where an animal lives

mammals—warm-blooded animals that have backbones and feed their young milk

mucus—a thick liquid that protects skin by keeping it moist

nocturnal—active at night

nostrils—the two openings of the nose

submerged—completely underwater

tusks—long, pointed teeth

wallow—to roll in mud or water

To Learn More

AT THE LIBRARY

Hansen, Grace. *Hippopotamus*. Minneapolis, Minn.: ABDO Kids, 2018.

Heos, Bridget. *Do You Really Want to Meet a Hippopotamus?* Mankato, Minn.: Amicus Ink, 2017.

Riggs, Kate. *Hippopotamuses*. Mankato, Minn.: Creative Education, 2016.

ON THE WEB

FACTSURFER

Factsurfer.com gives you a safe, fun way to find more information.

1. Go to www.factsurfer.com.

2. Enter "hippopotamuses" into the search box and click 🔍.

3. Select your book cover to see a list of related web sites.

Index

The images in this book are reproduced through the courtesy of: Sergey Uryadnikov, front cover, p. 4; Krista Rossow/ Getty Images, p. 6; JMx Images, p. 7; Angyalosi Beata, p. 8; mountainpix, p. 9; jeep2499, p. 9 (bottom); Agfa Wildlife/ Alamy, p. 10; Kakuli, p. 11; Phillip Allaway, p. 12; Amitrane, p. 13; GM Photo Images/ Alamy, p. 14; Stuart G Porter, p. 15; Claude Huot, p. 16; Jeroen van den Broek, p. 17; wilddog, p. 18; Mithlesh Kumari, p. 19 (top left); Snehalata, p. 19 (top right); RukiMedia, p. 19 (bottom); Anton_Ivanov, p. 20; Albie Venter, p. 21; Ondrej Prosicky, p. 23.